Number the pictures in **1**, **2**, **3** order to show what happens **first**, **next**, and **last**.

_____ _____ _____

Most birds can fly.

fact   opinion

Add the letters that make the verb **past tense**.

The cat jump_____ _____ down.

Where is Sam going?

to swim   to play baseball

In which season is this holiday?

winter   fall   summer

Circle the **odd** numbers.

52   47   25   12

18   13   39

Circle **true** or **false**.

Birds have feathers.

true   false

Snakes are reptiles.

true   false

Insects have **4** legs.

true   false

Tadpoles become turtles.

true   false

Which word **rhymes** with **mouse**?

horse   house

What day comes **before** Friday?

Monday   Sunday   Thursday

What time is it?

8:00   8:30   8:15

Circle **2** words that have the same **vowel sound** as **tie**.

pie   kite   pig

Count the dimes by **10**'s. Write the amount.

_____ ¢

Circle the **noun** in the sentence.

An elephant is big.

Which shape is a **triangle**? Trace.

Write the words in **ABC** order.
bird   dog   cat

_____

_____

_____

Which word has the **same meaning** as **stop**?

begin   end

Who had lunch **first**? Circle.

Mother had lunch at 1:00 PM.

Anna had lunch at 12:00 PM.

Bobby had lunch at 12:30 PM.

How many ears do **3** rabbits have **in all**?

2 + 2 + 2 = _____

Say the word. How many **syllables** do you hear?

butterfly

1   2   3

How much money is there?

10¢   9¢   7¢

Write the **compound** word.

_____

Which word begins with the **same sound** as **soap**?

Circle the things that are alive.

Which gift is on the **bottom**?

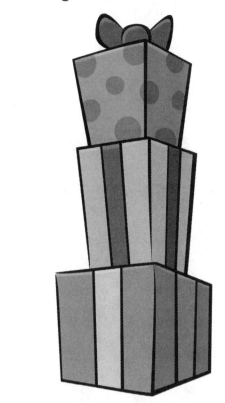

How many more baseballs do you need to have **10** baseballs?

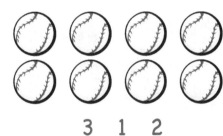

3   1   2

Circle the word that is the **opposite** of **over**.

after   under

before

7 sheep are in the pen. **5** sheep are in the yard. How many more sheep are in the pen?

_____ sheep

Amy picked **2** more apples than **4**. How many did she pick?

6   5   2

How many months are in a year?

10   11   12

Circle the animal in the **middle**.

Write the missing symbol.

+ –

$5\_\_5=0$

$5\_\_5=10$

Finish the word **pattern**.

sad happy sad happy sad _____

What **3** things do plants need to grow?

water   clouds   soil   sun

Which clown is **taller**?

How many nickels are in a dime?

2 nickels   3 nickels

What do you use to measure **weight**?

clock   thermometer   scale

Which shape does **not belong**?

Circle the **verb** in the sentence.

Jake hit the ball.

Which object is a **cylinder**?

What measures **temperature**?

Circle the **5 vowels** in the alphabet.

a b c d

e f g h

i j k l m

n o p q

r s t u v

w x y z

Change the first letter in hat to make **2** new words.

_____ at   _____ at

The cookie costs **20¢**.
Can you buy it?

yes   no

8

Count by **5**'s. Fill in the missing numbers.

5   10 _____ 20 _____ 30 _____ 40

60 _____ 70   75 _____ 85 _____ 95

What does this sentence **mean**?

Don't bug me!

Don't _____ me.

bother   forget

The movie starts at **5:00 PM**.
It is **2** hours long. At what time
does the movie end?

_____ o'clock

How many miles is it from Ferry to Perry?

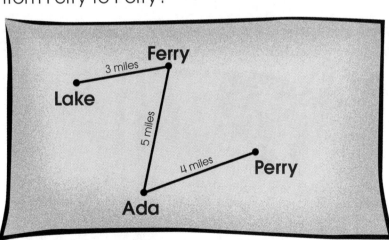

_____ miles

Underline the words that need a **capital** letter.

sara named her puppy pal.

Which **vowel sound** does the letter **Y** have in these pictures?

i   e

Where is the pot of gold?

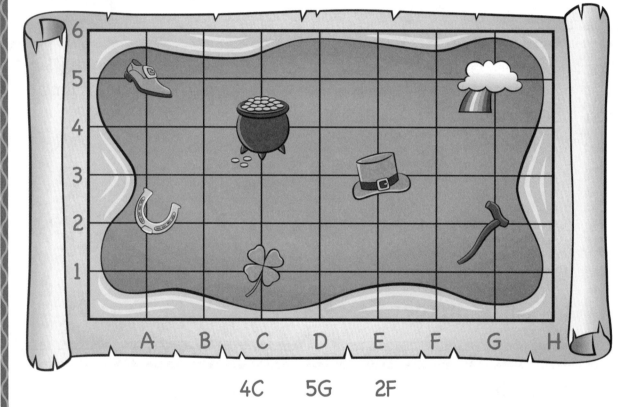

4C   5G   2F

Whales are ____.

fish   mammals

Which is bigger?

a town   a city

Which word is the **opposite** of easy?

The test was ___.

hard   simple

Cross out the word that does **not belong**.

foot   hand   home   leg

Which word means **more than 1** leaf?

leafs   leaves

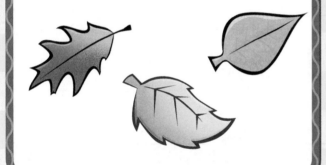

Circle the word that connects the two sentences.

I have a cat.
I have a dog.

I have a cat and a dog.

Circle two words that **rhyme**.

van   plane   train

Do these words have the **short** or **long e** sound?

seal   tree   key

long e   short e

Which word has the **same meaning** as **start**?

It is time to ____ the race.

end   begin

The Earth is a ____.

sphere   circle

Count by **2**'s. Fill in the missing numbers.

2 4 ____ ____ ____ ____ 14

24 ____ 28 30 ____ 34 ____ 38

Add the letter that makes **bug** mean **more than 1** bug.

bug____

Add the letter that makes **flower** mean **more than 1** flower.

flower____

How many hamburgers were eaten? Count the **tally marks**.

|||| |||| |||| |||| |||| ||

____

How much time would it take you to eat a hot dog?

5 hours   15 minutes

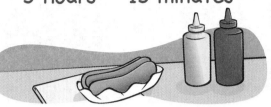

What number is in the **tens** place?

145 _____

224 _____

Circle the pictures that have the "**or**" sound.

Which clock has the **minute** hand on **5**?

Which word means **there is**?

_____ room for one more.

There's   Theirs

Do these pictures **rhyme**?

yes   no

Circle the shape that fits.

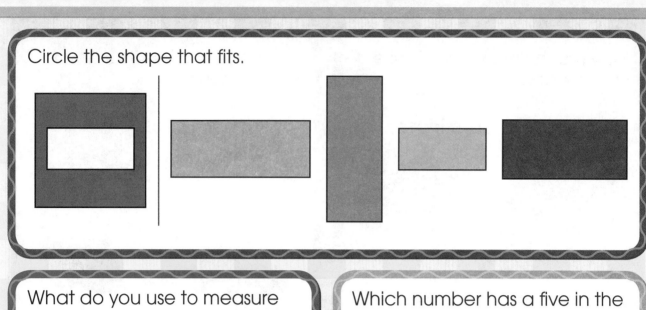

What do you use to measure **volume**?

calendar

ruler

measuring cup

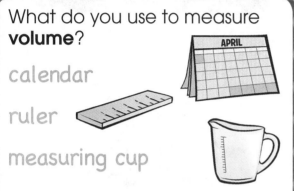

Which number has a five in the **ones** place?

27 52 59

14 63 25

Circle the **noun** in the sentence.

My sister is six.

Which word has the same **beginning sound** as **thirty**?

30

think   train

Draw and color the missing shape to complete the **pattern**.

Circle the objects you can roll.

Circle the pictures that have the "**ir**" sound.

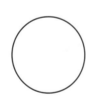 

Order the numbers from the **least** to the **greatest**.

54 18 63 31

___ ___ ___ ___

Which word **describes** snow?

Snow is _____.

cold   sharp

Is there enough money to buy the item?

55¢ _____ _____ _____

yes

no

Frogs begin life in _____.

water   trees

Circle the pictures that have the "**ow**" sound.

In which season do leaves fall from the trees?

winter   fall   summer

Fill in the letters **ed** to make **3** action words **past tense**.

p	a	i	n	t		
				a		
				n		
				c		
p	l	a	y			

What number is **greater**?

61

forty-six

Which clock shows **12:30**?

Color **10** balls. How many **are left**?

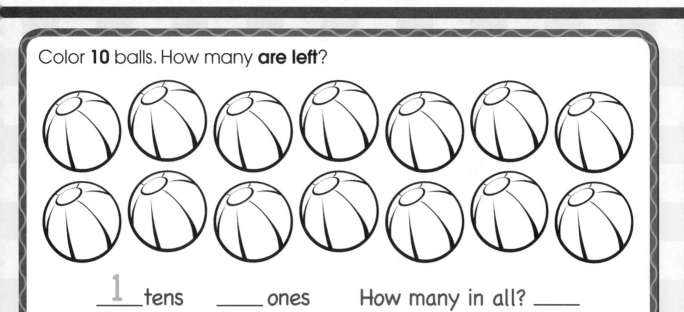

___1___ tens _____ ones   How many in all? _____

Is there enough money to buy the item?

yes   no

Birds are pretty.

fact   opinion

Dogs are pets.

fact   opinion

Sally bought **5** toy boats. Check the boxes she bought.

Which **vowel sound** do you hear in **tube**?

long u   short u

Which **sense** is being used?

touch   taste   hear

Which kind of pet does Pat like?   _____

Which kind of pet does Carl like?   _____

Which kind of pet does Jamar like?   _____

dog   **both**   **cat**

Sam   Justin

Chad   Kate

Jamar

Janet

Pat   Carl

Kayla   Tamara

Can you see air?

yes   no

Do these pictures **rhyme**?

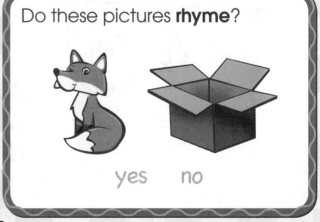

yes   no

Cross out the word that does **not** belong.

book

ruler

pencil

taco

Make words that begin with **ch**. Draw a line from the word to the picture word.

____ ____ick

____ ____erry

____ ____air

Which word begins with the **soft** "c" sound in city?

cent   candy

Circle the picture that shows $\frac{2}{3}$ of the pizza colored.

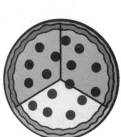

Circle **true** or **false**.

Insects can fly.

true   false

A plant is alive.

true   false

Write a word that finishes the sentences.

I _____ popcorn.

I do not _____ peas.

Which word means the
opposite of **empty**?

full   wide

Which shape is a **cube**?

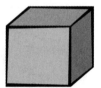

sunny										
rainy										
cloudy										

0   1   2   3   4   5   6   7   8   9   10

Number of Days

How many days are sunny ? _____

How many days are rainy ? _____

How many days are cloudy ? _____

Write the **difference**.

$$10 \quad\quad 24 \quad\quad 36$$
$$\underline{-\ 7} \quad\quad \underline{-\ 2} \quad\quad \underline{-\ 4}$$

Shoes are to feet as mittens
are to _____.

hands   boots

20

Which **2** pictures **rhyme**?

Which **plural** word for **penny** is correct?

pennies   pennys

Number the pictures in **1, 2, 3** order to show what happens **first**, **next**, and **last**.

_____

_____

_____

Circle the correct end mark.

Can you come with me

. ? !

_____

Ask your mother

. ? !

_____

Hurry and ask her now

. ? !

Which **odd** number comes after **7**?

10   9   11

_____

Which **odd** number comes after **16**?

17   18   20

Circle **true** or **false**.

An hour is 60 minutes.

true   false

Count by **5**'s. Fill in the missing numbers.

5 _____ 15 _____ 25 _____ 35 _____

Circle the **noun** in the sentence.

The dog ran away.

Which **sense** is being used?

touch   taste   hear

Which weighs **more than** a pound?

stamp   mouse   pumpkin

Write a **shorter** way to say the sentence.

I can not hear you.

I _____ hear you.

Which one hopped the **shortest** distance?

22

Is there enough money to buy the item?

yes

no

30¢ _____ _____ _____ _____ _____

Which clock has the **hour hand** on **9**?

Circle the **verb** in the sentence.

The bird flew away.

Circle **true** or **false**.
Dinosaurs are extinct.

true   false

The winning number is between **40** and **50**.
Circle the person with the winning card.

Circle **true** or **false**.

Insects begin life as eggs.

true   false

It's a home run! What sport is it?

soccer   baseball

Circle who is in the **middle**.

Add **st** to make a word.
Draw a line from the word
to the picture word.

_____ ar

_____ op

_____ ing

_____ ool

_____tens   _____ ones

How many 🐞s? _____

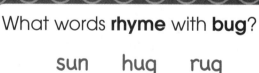

What words **rhyme** with **bug**?

sun   hug   rug

Count by **10's**. Fill in the missing numbers.

10 20 _____ 40 50 _____ 70 _____ 90

100 _____ 120 _____ 140 _____ 160

Which shape has **4** equal sides? Trace.

square   rectangle

Which mark do you put at the end of a **telling** sentence?

It is a cloudy day

.   ?   !

Write the numbers. Write **<** or **>** in the circle to show which is **greater**.

_____   ( )   _____

Count the money.

15¢   20¢   25¢

Circle the correct spelling.

Who _____ the game?

one   won

Fill in the last column of the graph. The first one is done for you.

Fish Caught		
Children	**Number of Fish:** 🐟 **= 2 fish**	**Number of Fish**
Tom	🐟 🐟 🐟	6
Abby	🐟 🐟 🐟 🐟 🐟	
Tia	🐟	
Sam	🐟 🐟	
Alex	🐟 🐟 🐟 🐟	

How many days are in a week?

6   5   7

Which word has the **same sound** as **new**?

bus   blue

Order the numbers from the **least** to the **greatest**.

12   10   15   13

____ ____ ____ ____

19   29   16   25

____ ____ ____ ____

Circle two words that **rhyme**.

whale   car   snail

Which word is the **opposite** of **open**?

Mr. Adams ____ the door.

closed   locked

8 cats are on your bed.
2 jump off.

How many are left on your bed?

____

Circle **true** or **false**.

The sun gives us heat and light.

true   false

Underline the **describing** word in the sentence.

I saw three goats.

Phone begins with which letter sound?

p   f

Write the missing letter to make two words.

	E	A	R
E			
A			
N			

Which snake is the **longest**?

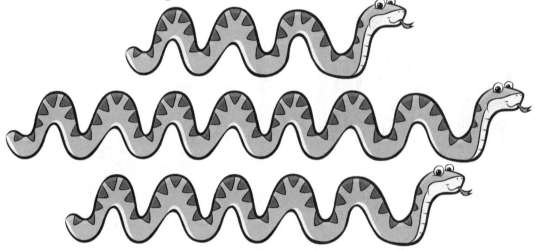

Which picture begins with **fl**?

Circle the matching time.

 5:00    3:00

What can you **taste**?

What time of the year is it?

winter   summer

Write the number of corners.
Check the shape that has **more**.

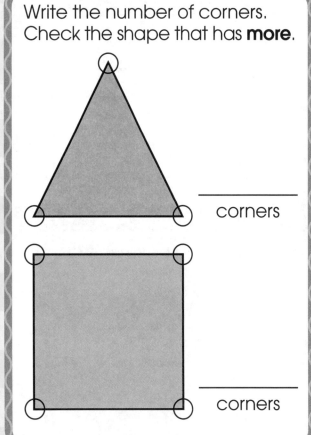

_____ corners

_____ corners

Which word is the **opposite** of **front**?

back   before

Which word **describes** a kitten?

A kitten is very _____.

soft   hard

Which word has the **same sound** as **toy**?

ball   boy

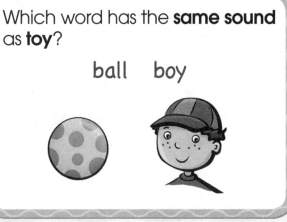

Use the code to write words for the clues.

Code

A	D	M	O	P	U
△	□	○	☆	○	□

How much of the pizza was eaten?

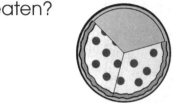

$\frac{1}{4}$ $\frac{1}{2}$ $\frac{1}{3}$

Which shape is a **cone**?

Which word does **not belong**?

hop   jump   happy   run

Which weighs **more than** a pound?

Write the time.

_____   _____   _____

Which one is **not** a square?

Which picture begins with the **soft "g"** sound in **gym**?

Circle the **compound word** these two pictures make.

starfish   goldfish

Which number is **greater**?

54   64

_____

68   86

Draw and color the missing picture to complete the **pattern**.

   _____

Little Thinkers First Grade

Make a word that **rhymes** with **net**.

____et

Which word **describes** a mouse?

tiny   long

Say the word. How many **syllables** do you hear?

monkey

1   2   3

elephant

1   2   3

Mike has **10** marbles. Jack gave him **10** more.

How many does he have **in all**?

20   25   30

Underline the words that need a **capital letter**.

susan and jan are friends.

Circle the **verb** in the sentence.

Jackson walked to school.

Circle **real** or **fantasy**.

The cow jumped over the moon.

real　　　fantasy

Jenny fed the cow hay.

real　　　fantasy

Fish make good pets.

fact　　　opinion

Add the letters that make the verb **past tense**.

The ball roll_____ _____ away.

Write the numbers from **smallest** to **largest**.

30	17	8	41		18	10	29	12
___	___	___	___		___	___	___	___
115	90	76	112		48	56	39	42
___	___	___	___		___	___	___	___

In which season is this holiday?

winter   fall   summer

Circle the **even** numbers.

17   30   32

12

6   11   28

Write the **short vowel a, e, i, o,** or **u** to finish each word.

h___t   p___g   r___g   c___t

b___x   b___d   b___s   w___b

Circle the word that means **more than one** mouse.

mouses   mice

What day comes **after** Monday?

Sunday   Thursday   Tuesday

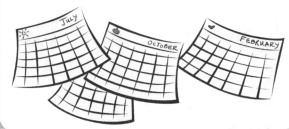

What does this sentence mean?

It's a piece of cake.

It is easy.   It is sweet.

Write the words in **ABC** order.

Jill   Beth   Haley   Anna

_____

_____

_____

_____

How many minutes in an hour?

60   30

_____

How many minutes in a half hour?

45   30

A **noun** names a person, place, or thing. Circle the noun.

Our car is red.

How much time would it take?

50 minutes   50 days

Circle the correct **contraction**.

It_____ snowing now.

isn't   aren't

Which word is the **opposite** of **under**?

beside   over

_____

Which word is the **opposite** of **hot**?

cold   heavy

Draw a **triangle** using the dots.

Say each word. Draw a line to the **long vowel** sound.

bee

tube

cake

kite

boat

a   e   i   o   u

Circle the correct word.

Doug and ____ are friends

me   I

How much money is there?

36¢   46¢   26¢

Write the **compound** word.

 +

_____

Circle the animals that are insects.

Circle the **setting**.

The bell rang.
Recess was over.

at school   at home

How many are there?

38 ____tens ____ones

83 ____tens ____ones

64 ____tens ____ones

23 ____tens ____ones

39 ____tens ____ones

6 kids were on the bus.
3 more got on.
How do you find how many are on the bus now?

add   subtract

How many eggs are in a dozen?

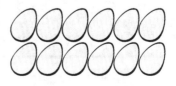

10   12

Lily looked up and down the aisle. She still has not found a can of beans. Circle the **setting**.

a bakery

a grocery store

A pet store

Sam caught **4 more** fish than **5**. How many did he catch?

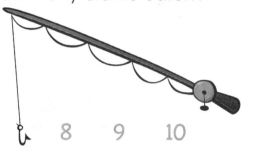

8   9   10

Circle **true** or **false**.

There are four seasons in a year.

true   false

Circle the word that is the **opposite** of fast.

slow   quick

Write the missing symbol.

$+$ $-$

9 ___ 7 = 2

9 ___ 3 = 12

How many inches long is the snake?

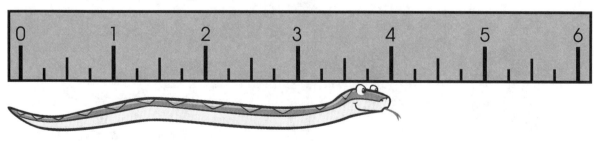

_____ inches

Fill in the missing numbers.

79 _____ 81 _____ 83 _____ 85 _____

105 _____ 107 _____ 109 _____ 111 _____

Circle the pictures that end with the "**er**" sound.

How many nickels are in a quarter?

4 nickels   5 nickels

Which weighs **less than** a pound?

There are **9** players on a baseball team.
How many **more** players are needed? _____

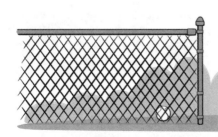

Circle the **verb** in the sentence.

My brother plays in the park.

Which object is a **cube**?

Say the word. How many **syllables** do you hear?

suitcase

1   2   3

octopus

1   2   3

Follow the path of **even** numbers.

start

2	85	11	93	79	37	5
4	6	8	10	12	14	23
7	63	37	13	49	16	69
31	65	24	22	20	18	43
1	27	26	87	99	53	81
75	33	28	30	27	11	9
57	61	89	32	49	73	25
97	38	36	34	19	95	23
77	40	42	44	46	48	50

finish

Circle the shape that has **equal** parts.

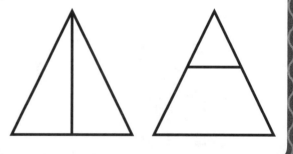

The cookie costs **40¢**. Can you buy it?

yes   no

Balloons cost **2¢** each. How much do **5** toys cost?

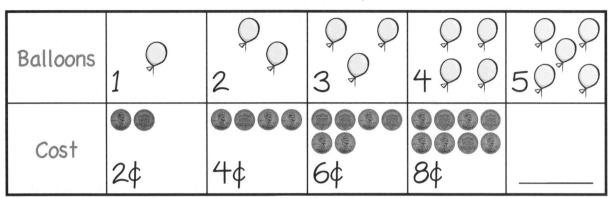

Balloons	1	2	3	4	5
Cost	2¢	4¢	6¢	8¢	_____

5 toys cost _____.

Circle **true** or **false**.

A fact is something that is true.

true   false

Equal means **the same**.

true   false

The game begins at **1:30**.
It is **1** hour long. At what time does the game end?

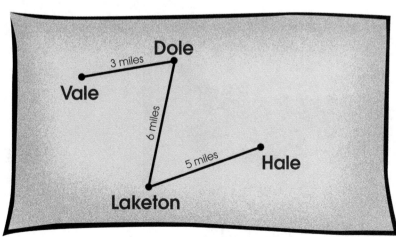

2:30   3:30

How many miles is it from Vale to Hale?

Dole

3 miles

Vale

6 miles

5 miles   Hale

Laketon

_____ miles

Underline the words that need a **capital** letter.

jan's birthday is may 15.

Circle the **long a** word.

night   day

Use the calendar to answer the questions.

How many days make a week? _____

What day begins each week? _____

On what day does this month begin? _____

Alligators are _____.

reptiles   mammals

Circle the **beginning sound**.

sk   sl   sn

Is this a complete sentence?

Frog in pond.

yes   no

Cross out the word that does **not belong**.

run   walk   bird   swing

_____

hat   socks   jeans   pie

Circle the correct **plural** ending.

I like _____.

cherries   cherrys

Underline the **descriptive** word in each sentence.

Lady is a big cat.

Lady had three kittens.

Write the correct end mark.

Can you come with me _____

.   ?   !

Circle the correct word to complete the sentence.

The wind _____ it away.

blue   blew

Henry _____ the answer.

knew   new

Which word has the **same meaning** as **little**?

large   small

_____

Which word has the **same meaning** as **happy**?

glad   small

Circle **true** or **false**.

Our sun is a star.

true   false

Ocean water is salty.

true   false

Tennis balls cost **5¢** each. How much do **6** balls **cost**?

Tennis Balls	1	2	3	4	5	6
Cost	5¢	10¢	15¢	20¢	_____	_____

6 tennis balls cost _____.

Underline the correct spelling.

The rabbit is ____ away.

hopping   hoping

The baby is ____.

naping   napping

Circle **true** or **false**.

A **noun** names a person, place, or thing.

true   false

An **adjective** is a describing word.

true   false

How much time would it take to bake a cake?

1 hour   10 minutes

What number is in the **tens** place?

179 _____

230 _____

Circle the pictures that have the "**ou**" sound.

Circle the cone **shape**.

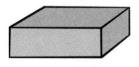

Circle **true** or **false**.

A **verb** is an action word.

true   false

Circle the correct word to complete the sentence.

I do not ____ the answer.

no   know

Draw and color the missing shape to complete the **pattern**.

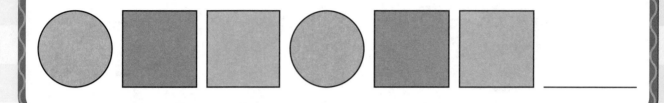

_____

What do you use to measure **length**?

ruler

calendar

measuring cup

Which numbers have a seven in the **tens** place?

80   17   45

70   75   175

Circle the **noun** in the sentence.

Our car is old.

Circle the number that comes **before**.

27

25   29   26

Order the numbers from the **smallest** to the **largest**.

36   75   23   48   91   67   43   12

___   ___   ___   ___   ___   ___   ___   ___

Draw hands on the clocks to show the movie times.

Daffy Dino 1:30   Cats in Space 2:45   Mystery Mouse 5:15

Draw a line through the **long i** words.

fish	find	book
out	fly	his
kick	right	you

Circle the **beginning sound**.

sl   sh   sk

Which **length** of time is longer?

minutes   seconds

Write the next number to continue the **pattern**.

3   4   5   3   4   5   _____

Circle **true** or **false**.

Most plants begin from seeds.

true   false

In which season does it snow?

summer   winter   fall

Write the beginning letters to make **long o** words.

____old

____old

____old

Circle the words that have the **vowel sound** in **moon**.

zoo

bug

soon

flew

new

fun

Which number is **less**?

82

forty-five

Circle **true** or **false**.

There are **24** letters in the alphabet.

true   false

How many **tens** and **ones**?

_____tens _____ones How many in all? _____

Jack had **8¢**.
He spent **5¢**.
How much does he have now?

_____¢

Spiders are scary.

fact   opinion

_____

Spiders have **8** legs.

fact   opinion

$\frac{1}{2}$ of the dogs are inside.

$\frac{1}{2}$ of the dogs are outside.

How many dogs are there in all? _____

Which word has the **short o** sound?

box   boat   bone

Which **sense** is being used.

touch   smell   hear

Who is on **top**?
Read the clues.

King is on the bottom.

Spot is in the middle.

Hero is under Max.

Where is Mia?

_____

_____

_____

_____

_____

Circle the **verb** in the sentence.

Squirrels climb trees.

Add the letters that make the verb **past tense**.

Bob laugh_____ _____ at her joke.

Circle the word that best **describes** the things listed.

coins money

Circle the **noun** in each sentence.

The pony is hungry.

The pail is empty.

Underline the correct spelling.

David is _____.

jogging joging

What shape is this?

cone sphere cube

Circle **true** or **false**.

Air is found only outside.

true false

Ice is frozen water.

true false

Write the correct answer.
There are **5** birds **in all**.

How many can't be seen? _____

Which word means the **opposite** of **before**?

after   last

_____

Which word means the **opposite** of **tall**?

short   little

Circle the **rectangle**.

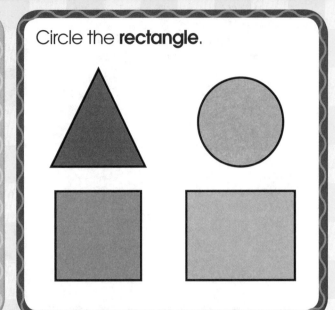

David										
Jan										
Ken										

0 1 2 3 4 5 6 7 8 9 10

Boxes of Cookies

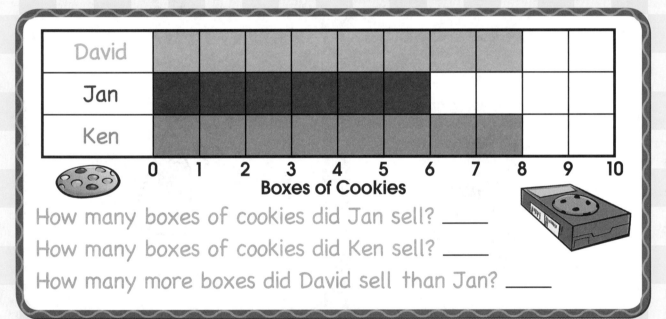

How many boxes of cookies did Jan sell? _____

How many boxes of cookies did Ken sell? _____

How many more boxes did David sell than Jan? _____

What time is it?

3:30   3:45   2:45

Circle the word that has the **same sound**.

house   town

Which word has the **long i** sound?

fish   pig   pie

A **plural** word means **more than one**.

true   false

Number the pictures in **1**, **2**, **3** order to show what happens **first**, **next**, and **last**.

_____

_____

_____

Circle the correct word to finish the sentence.

The dogs _____ barking.

is   are

The cat _____ sleeping.

is   are

The pigs _____ eating.

is   are

The rooster _____ crowing.

is   are

Which **even** number comes after **68**?

72 69 70

Which **even** number comes after **78**?

80 83 85

What is a **shorter** way to say **did not**?

didn't   don't

What is a **shorter** way to say **is not**?

isn't   aren't

Circle the correct number sentence.

6+2=8   5+2=7   7+2=9

Underline the proper **noun** in the sentence.

Give Grandmother her gift.

Underline the word that means the **same** as **all**.

every   some

Underline the word that means the **same** as **slip**.

push   slide

Circle the one that is **lighter**.

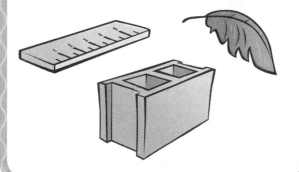

Circle the correct word to finish the sentence.

Doug has ____ sisters.

for   four

Susan found **12** shells.
7 shells broke.
How many does she have left?

____ shells

Circle the **fifth** child in line.

Which thermometer shows the outside **temperature**?

°F
100
90
80
70
60
50
40
30
20
10
0
-10

°F
100
90
80
70
60
50
40
30
20
10
0
-10

°F
100
90
80
70
60
50
40
30
20
10
0
-10

Circle the **verb** in the sentence.

The ball bounced high.

Circle the **long i** word that ends in **y**.

fly   baby

Anna spent **12¢**
What did she buy?

8¢   5¢   2¢   4¢

Circle **true** or **false**.

Our heart pumps blood around our body.

true   false

He made a touchdown. What sport is it?

soccer   football

Write the answers to the subtraction problems.

Subtract 2	
16 _____	19 _____
20 _____	15 _____
33 _____	68 _____
82 _____	97 _____

Add **sh** to make a word. Draw a line from the word to the picture word.

_____ ip

_____ ell

_____ irt

_____ eep

What number is **more**?

65
ninety-five

Circle the correct word.

Put the book over _____.

there   their

Number the stages of a frog's life cycle.

_____   _____   _____   _____   _____

What is a **shorter** way to say **do not**?

don't   didn't

_____

What is a **shorter** way to say **can not**?

can't   isn't

Write the mark you put at the end of an **asking** sentence.

How are you _____

. ? !

Number the sentences from **1** to **4** to show the **order**.

_____ Then the seeds were planted.

_____ Finally, there were pretty flowers.

_____ Mother bought flower seeds.

_____ Plants began to grow.

Which coin is worth **10** pennies?

Circle the correct spelling.

Let's stop _____.

hear   here

Write **C** in front of the sentence that tells the **cause**.
Write **E** in front of the sentence that tells the **effect**.

_____ The pancakes were burned.

_____ The pan was too hot.

_____ It was a hot day.

_____ The ice pop melted.

_____ The game got canceled.

_____ It was raining.

Dan is **2** years younger than Ben.
Ben is **9** years old.
How old is Dan?

_____

Solve the problem.

$$10 - 2$$ $$18 - 5$$

Circle the picture that shows $\frac{1}{4}$ of the pie colored.

Circle **true** or **false**.

Bees make honey.

true   false

All birds fly.

true   false

Which word has the **same meaning** as **fast**?

quick   start

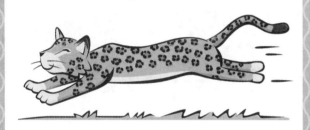

8 bugs are on the leaf.
2 more land.
How many bugs are there now?

_____

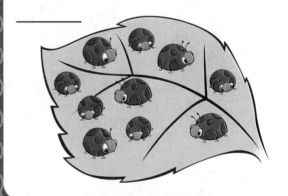

Circle the amount that is **less**.

Underline the **describing** word.

Steven has a white rabbit.

Which word has the **short o** sound?

fox   boat   snow

Circle the fraction.

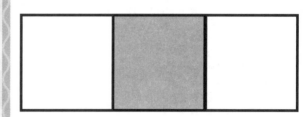

$\frac{1}{2}$ $\frac{1}{3}$ $\frac{1}{4}$

Number the pictures from **1** to **4** to show the **order**.

_____   _____   _____   _____

Write the **odd** number that comes next.

1 3 5 7 _____

Write the **even** number that comes next.

2 4 6 8 _____

Circle **true** or **false**.

He and she are pronouns.

true   false

Christmas is in November.

true   false

Circle **true** or **false**.

Moving air is wind.

true   false

Trees are the largest plants.

true   false

Write the correct answers.

How many sides?

_____

How many corners?

_____

How many square corners?

_____

What time of year is it?

Jan lost her mittens.

summer   winter   fall

Circle the correct word to complete the sentences.

Wen and Josh _____ taking the bus.

          is   are

Dani _____ walking to school.

          is   are

Wen and Josh _____ friends

          is   are

Write a number sentence. Tim lost **3** of his pencils.

How many does he have left?

8 PENCILS

_____ − _____ = _____

What would you use to measure the **length** of a table?

Circle the correct word to complete the sentences.

Jack hides in bed during thunderstorms. Jack is _____.

tired   afraid

Brad's pet rabbit won first prize. Brad is _____.

proud   bored

9 cherries were on a tree.
2 fell off.

How do you find how many are left?

add   subtract

Circle the **beginning sound**.

dr   br   cr

Which word **does not** belong?

under   better   over   inside

Pam is reading a note and smiling.

Pam is _____.

happy   surprised

Write a number sentence.

 **+**

_____ **+** _____ **=** _____

Write the next number to continue the **pattern**.

8   4   4   8   4   4   _____

Say the word. How many **syllables** do you hear?

apple

1   2   3

pineapple

1   2   3

Write the words in **ABC** order.

zebra   zero   zoo

_____

_____

_____

Write the number that comes **before**.

____ 38

____ 42

____ 54

Circle the correct word to complete the sentences.

Fanny _____ at the funny joke.

cried   giggled

Brad _____ the race.

won   one

Circle **true** or **false**.

The letters **a**, **e**, **i**, **o**, and **u** are vowels.

true   false

There are **long** and **short** vowels.

true   false

Circle the correct **contraction**.

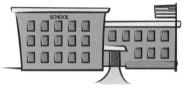

School _____ started yet.

hasn't   haven't

Draw lines to **match** the shapes.

Draw a line to the problems that **equal** the number **11**.

6+5   3+7

11

8+3   4+7

6+3   9+2

Circle the correct spelling.

The soup is _____ hot to eat.

to   too

Max has **5** marbles.
2 are blue.
2 are green.
How many are orange?

5   1   0